To Claim Loneliness

poems by

Doris Ferleger

Finishing Line Press
Georgetown, Kentucky

To Claim Loneliness

*With deepest gratitude for my parents,
Miriam Ferleger, z"l, and Avram Ferleger, z"l,
who, after sustaining countless devastations
of the Holocaust, brought with them
from the Old County, all they had learned
from their families: abiding love, resilience,
kinship, humor, curiosity, a remarkable ability
for forgiveness and a profound gratitude for being alive.
These things, no one could take from them.*

Copyright © 2023 by Doris Ferleger
ISBN 979-8-88838-311-7 First Edition
All rights reserved under International and Pan-American Copyright Conventions. No part of this book may be reproduced in any manner whatsoever without written permission from the publisher, except in the case of brief quotations embodied in critical articles and reviews.

Publisher: Leah Huete de Maines
Editor: Christen Kincaid
Cover Art: Nalewki Photography
Author Photo: Larmon Studio
Cover Design: Elizabeth Maines McCleavy

Order online: www.finishinglinepress.com
also available on amazon.com

Author inquiries and mail orders:
Finishing Line Press
P. O. Box 1626
Georgetown, Kentucky 40324
U. S. A.

Table of Contents

Part 1

Rivers 1
Lifeline 2
Thank You, Momma 3
Tashlich (Casting Away) 5
Conversations with My Grown Son 1742 Miles Away 7
Momma Tells Me How 10
Urge to Be 13
Love Letter from Time 14
Be Happy and Never Forget 15
Stone for a Pillow 17
Pillowless 18
Winter Sun in My Son's Room 20
Momma Would Say *Sara* or *Hella*, Then Turn 21
Last Generation 22
One moment my life is a stone in me, the next, a star 23
Stone Prophecy Says 24

Part 2

Enough Lament 27
Poppa 28
Memorial Flame 30
Why I Hate the Word "Horrible" When Used for Less Than 34
Never Alone 35
First Taste of Salt 37
Somersault Solo at the Senior Expressive Arts Center 38
Nothing Is Everything 40
Leepah 41
Shoppers Guide for the Vilnius Flea Market 42
The Brain and All Its Parts 44
The Egg Trick 46
Momma Speaks of Her Father, Leepah 48
Summer Says 49
There Is the Smell 50
At Ghost Ranch 51
Notes 53
Acknowledgements 54

Part 1

That we will die is perhaps the most interesting thing about us—and makes for compassion. —Ross Gay

Rivers

When asked my birthplace,
I name the wrong country.

I say *Shoah, Majdanek, shtetl.*
I have taken on the names

of rivers and the bottoms of rivers
belonging to those I loved, who loved me.

River stones fell into my pockets.
River waters sustained me.

Now I lean beneath maples
and listen to the birdcalls

and the spaces between birdcalls,
between trees and the river,

between the river
and the source of all rivers.

Lifeline

I can't imagine Momma ever claiming loneliness.
Momma, with telephone receiver in hand, and two
surviving sisters on the other end of the line,
at least five times a day back when party lines
let them listen-in on strangers' conversations—
which could have been about private parts or potato
soup recipes. Momma and her sisters—who propped
each other up in the roll call lines of Bergen Belsen,
Auschwitz, Majdanek—were never alone as long
as they held the phone receiver in their hands—
until the husbands came home from work
and the chicken baked a beautiful bronze.

Thank You, Momma

for the time I lost my math book or at least couldn't find it in the canary-yellow
kitchen or under the orange-crushed-velvet couch—you, so crazy about color
and jungle wild floral print dresses you'd sweet-talk

me into trying on, saying, *tak wadneh, so pretty, you look,* then spit
between your fingers right in the fitting room though no spit came out, wasn't
meant to, just the gesture made me safe from the evil eye—

when I asked if you'd seen it, you said straight-faced, *I saw five men running
down the street "mit" such a book, so heavy it looked, all doze problems, adding,
multiplying.*

And thank you, Momma for the absence note you brought to school though it
made Mrs. Wexler call me a liar right in the middle of *dodgeball*, game I never
understood, or thought was just plain mean,

and you told her, *Mein daughter is not a liar, just a person who wants to be
perfect.* And just after when I ran across the playground to throw
up in the little girls' room, nerves akimbo, thank you for running after

me and holding my head—and before piano lessons with Mr. Littman who
popped sen-sens, those tiny red diamond-shaped-breath-mints into his mouth
a million times a minute, did you know I thought they were

nerve pills, believed my piano practice was so poor it got on his nerves?
Thank you, Momma, for telling him not to come anymore.
I am trying to thank you for not speaking enough English for me to feel

safe in the streets and for how you learned to read beside me, Dick,
Jane, and Spot, but never read to me—no *Charlotte's Web* or *Good Night Moon*,
yet you drove me, thank you, each Saturday morning to the public library,

though you never entered for yourself.
And I am trying to thank you for speaking your mother tongues mixed together
so I didn't know where Yiddish ended and Polish began, and this matters

because I am trying now to speak just Polish to Agata who
has become like a mother to me, even has your syntax, your sarcasm, your
smart sayings and finds my often-misplaced books and keys. And my pink

fuzzy sweater that makes me feel loved.
You see, I am still always losing things, so nothing has changed since you've
gone, except I have lost you too, and Poppa and my dear husband. And thank

you Momma, for singing that Hebrew song, *Kol
ha'olam kulo gesher tsar meh'od. All the world is just a narrow bridge.*
I am just now learning the second verse: *Veha ikar lo lifahed klal.*

The point is to not be afraid. I am trying to thank you for being so afraid.

Tashlich, Casting away

My son agrees to meet me on the footbridge
        after he's run and sweated for miles—

even lets me place on his head the sky-
        blue *kipa* I've stolen

from synagogue this morning
        and the two of us tear,

into uneven bits,
        the ritual bread I've brought

and toss into the creek the crusts
        of our afflictions—

a year's worth of what
        some call sins.

Creek waters course, carrying
        our regrets downstream

over sticks and stones.
        (I used to worry as a child

the fish might eat my sins
        and die.)

We recite the prayer of penance
        we each know, heart by heart,

year by year. This year he closes
        his eyes for a long time, then looks, amber

and intent, into mine—his deepest way
        of showing

sorrow for words spoken
as shards

that don't resemble a history—
  except sometimes

when the night winds toss terribly.
  and moonlight bellows

between branches—
  I imagine we live in a ruined house.

And I speak my regrets for words
  that surely dented

his heart. As a child he used to sing:
  Sticks and stones

may break my bones, but words
  will always hurt me.

Today, on the footbridge, on the first
  day of the Jewish New Year

without a living father, he says *September*
  is a grieving month,

and I say *perhaps it is grief that causes*
  discord—grief left

ungrieved—or is it fear
  of weeping—or a shame

of needing
  to know we are loved?

Conversations with My Grown Son 1742 Miles Away

My son says, *I can feel the pleasure*
    you get from speaking
        about this or that, but sometimes it seems

you go away. Into your own world. Don't notice
    I'm not with you. And I wonder if you know
        you do that

and it makes me feel lonely.
    And I say to my son, *Yes, sometimes I notice.*
        He nods.

Though it's not a face-to-face call.
    I can feel his nod. Imagine he's glad
        to have an ally in his take of me.

Though I wish I'd said to my son,
    I'm sorry you have felt left,
        lonely. It makes so much sense.
~

I say to my son, *Sometimes I want to apologize*
    for all I've done or said to hurt you.
        Or do I say, *I apologize for all the things*

I've done or said to hurt you?
    No matter. He says *Wow. I just felt a pang.*
        As if I were already a father,

with all best intentions of not hurting,
    yet knowing inevitably, my child
        will feel hurt by me.

I can imagine how you feel—the pang of it.

~

And, oh, these pandemic months have made me
    almost brave enough to say:
        in case I die soon and fast

please know—in addition to loving you
    I thank you for all you've taught me—
        especially for the times

you would ask for my silence
    while we sat in the same room
        together, the kitchen especially,

and you'd be just about to dive
    into a dinner plate full of delicious
        brown rice you'd cooked a quicker

new way, leaving the lid off, adding water
    over and over the long grains
        you've dusted with cumin and crushed

red peppers and maybe cinnamon,
    my tongue still determining the surprising
        flavor, and you'd proffer a perfect number

of spoons-full in a hand-painted little bowl,
    with red flowers at the bottom,
        the one bought in Italy,

because you know I like measured amounts
    at a time and because I am prone
        to tossing leftovers,

wasting food, which makes you more
    than cringe for the planet
        and its people.

Your Dad would be pleased I have finally
    followed his instructions
        on how to be with you

with more ease
	He used to say to me, *Try silence*
		as a way of being

with our son. Cook together. Taste
	what he has made. Say thank you
		for how quietly he shows his love.

Momma Tells Me How

> *I starve my belly for a sublime purpose/ I say to it: Belly,*
> *I am ashamed of you./ You must/spiritualize yourself. You must*
> *eat the sun.* —Anna Swir (Swierczynska)

Momma tells me how in the Warsaw Ghetto she built
a fire outside to cook rice for the twelve strangers

in her last hiding place. Doesn't mention cinders, smoke,
ash flying, buildings toppling, bombs dropping,

doesn't say she cooked as Warsaw burned and rubbled
all around them,

says one family sat and slept for days on the bags
of rice with hollow bellies waiting for who knows

when, I picture the mother in a beige sack dress,
dirty apron, the reluctant rising from a bag of rice

after Momma insisted for the last time, *or we will die.*
The sunken silence of my grandmother who'd stopped

speaking by then, a settled muteness of loss that lasted,
husband and other daughters already taken.

Momma tells me more often than I could stomach,
how she was always hungry. How she concocted

a song in *Majdanek* or was it *Auschwitz,* (does it matter?)
I won't give up my ration card, my ration card…

sung in nursery rhyme. I've kept re-memorizing
the names and order of the five, or was it six, camps

Momma starved in. She tells me meat got smuggled
into the ghetto in trash trucks, she sold bagels with a boy

days before re-finding her mother in the bunker.
I once read and reread the poems of Anna Swierczynska

who wrote of shivering in paper shoes with her father
in Warsaw's ration lines, and after, they'd go to the bombed-out

building where his art studio had been, each day,
they went as if the building would reappear

or was still standing there waiting for the war to end.
I read Milosz's commentary, Milosz, who loved and translated

Swir's poetry, though this little batch of her *Mother and Father* poems he
thought were simply sentimental tributes, and I wondered

how he missed that they were poems of war's obsessions, reenactments,
traumas, poems of a daughter's haunted inheritance. Inheritance of my

own hauntedness. If you were beside me now, I'd show you
Momma in the two smiling photos of her at fifteen, short bob of hair,

barretted on the left side as she barretted mine when I was a girl,
Momma hand in hand with her father on cobblestone

1935. Momma said her father slapped her only once in her life
because she asked for an ice cream cone.

In this other photo Momma holds hands with her sisters, same bob,
same white blouse, sisters who would be genocided four years later.

In the photo, they look happy and kind, outdoors on lean grasses
at a makeshift table, maybe a long wood board. Her father has

piercing eyes, uncut Orthodox beard, long *peyos*. I have no photos
of a smiling grandfather on either side. I can't keep count

how many times Momma repeats the story of Nazis finding her fire
Momma had made to cook the rice, how the soldiers threw tear gas inside

the bunker, how the fire betrayed them, how Momma's hunger
betrayed her— and though I know I should end here, I will tell you,

many years after Momma's death and ghost hungers and life stories
of times and places I could not go, though she took me to over and over,

I went to Poland, listened to Ed Hirsch recite a poem by Tadeusz
Rozewicz, Holocaust survivor: *this is a table I kept saying/this is a table/on*

*the table are bread knife/the knife is used for cutting bread/people feed on
bread/man should be loved/I learned by night by day/what should one love*

I answered man..../ Momma taught me how.

Urge to Be

Excerpts from Interview of our mother, Miriam Ferleger, by my brother, David Ferleger, 1998

I was with my friend, Abracza from Hashomer Hatzayir, a Zionist youth group, before the war. We were looking for my family who escaped to a bunker. We found them in a hiding place. I don't know how we found them. It was a house with a lot of people. This was the bunker with the rice. In the hiding place, people were sitting on rice and not sharing. I told them "we have to share. We are all hungry." So they shared. We tried to cook some rice outside. The Nazis, I guess, saw the smoke and found us. They put a gas bomb into the building, the bunker, and we ran out. This was the time we walked to the Umschlag which was a couple of hours. We were sleeping outside all night and in the morning, they put us in the train and we didn't know where we were going.

Love Letter from Time

I love the word *emergency*.
  Its redness, its lack of eventuality, its flash
    and crime. Its brothers—burn and rope.

I love the way humans startle,
  the jerk back of the body, the lunge forward.
    No sideways movements

come with emergency. No rhythmic beat or brush
  of drum begins it.
    Always the rigid riot.

Sometimes a pall of silence
  covers the body
    so it looks like the silvery sheet,

tissue light, tissue thin, is far less
  than volcanic.
    Emergency—

I like the evenness of its four syllables,
  how it takes too long
    to say it. By the time you say fire,

the house is rubble.
  By the time you say smoke,
    the sparrow, the tit-willow—

are hollowed out, featherless.

Be Happy and Never Forget—
If I can't forget, how can I be happy?

At kitchen table, over roasted chicken or Rice Crispies' snap, crackle, pop—never sure at what meal they'll turn up—aunts, grandparents, cousins—mentioned in casual conversation, how they were always hungry, or how they *were taken,* 128 genocided relatives to be exact, but who's counting, except my brother who has collected archives from the death camps, hand written lists, containing our last name, spelled by different scared, hungry hands, in different death camps, one slice of brown bread, one bowl of brown soup. At our kitchen table, the family's favorite delicacy: a thick piece bleached white bread, spread with sun yellow butter, sprinkled with Morton's salt from the blue container; see the happy girl in a yellow dress, twirling her big umbrella, protected from rain and death and any mention of *the camps.*

~

Summer camp. Day camp. Overnight camp. Never went. No place called *camp* could be safe.

~

Ach. Terrible shoes! Momma says of my new clogs. Though she can't say why. Until the next day when she says: *Oy, I know. Special shoes Nazis gave for death marches.*

~

4th of July fireworks—laughing mothers and fathers set out lawn chairs, spread blankets, packed picnic baskets, opened bottles of beer. My family sits on the dropped down rear door of our station wagon. Safely watching bombs bursting. Warsaw burning.

~

Momma teaches happiness is the opposite of dread. Happiness comes from feeling safe. Feeling safe comes from protecting her children from suffering. *We suffered enough so you shouldn't suffer*, Momma says. Suffering includes everything from a bruised knee, to feeling hungry, angry, tired, cold, hot or God forbid, spit between your fingers to avoid the evil eye, sad. To insure happy, safe children, Momma turns our house into a No Suffering Zone. Sends the square glass table top to get rounded so our little heads don't get cut on the sharp corners. Momma says don't go into the park. Crazy men escape from Byberry and hide there. Trying to create a sense of safety, Momma creates the dread she so wishes to free me from.

~

Thunderstorm. Momma gets that scared look, corners of her mouth turned down, then a fake smile, then she takes my child-sized, orange-handled scissors from my hand. I long to keep folding and cutting the red construction paper into a long row of connected paper dolls, to create the miracle of them joining hands and standing them up in a circle, the way Poppa shows me. But Momma says, *If the Holocaust could happen, anything can happen.* Meaning lightening could strike me dead if I'm holding the metal scissors and sitting in the living room, though it has no windows.

~

So down to the basement we go. In the basement Poppa built a very long bench that holds our *storm* toys, canned *storm* food and blankets. In his embroidery shop, Poppa stapled soft padding and sparkly green fabric on the bench and sewed cut-out faces of Mickey, Minnie, and Donald Duck across the front. We could sleep on the benches in case a storm lasts for days, or a Holocaust happens again. (When I am fifty, I will visit Auschwitz and see unpadded wooden benches Momma slept on, dreamt on.)

~

We stay at cheap motels where tacky knockoffs of Van Gogh's sun flowers hang over the beds. Momma swiftly removes the light weight pictures from the wall, the squares where the paint has not faded, and hooks are exposed. *If the Holocaust could happen, pictures can jump off walls.*

~

Poppa and I set up two green and white folding chairs with flimsy-mesh-crisscrossed slats, the kind that keep the impression of your bottom long after you stand up. Poppa talks about his life in the *Old Country.* When he does this, it is my *Old Country* too. He says, Dobcha, his mother, my namesake, was a *bren, a fireball.* Smart and quick, she made doll furniture from chicken bones. Poppa's family kitchen was also a restaurant. *Dobcha would say to a customer, Sure we have schnapps. Then she would run next door to borrow the "bissel" schnapps she didn't really have.*

~

My wife never feeds me, Poppa says to the waiter who sees him pocket the last two rolls from the breadbasket. Bread—Poppa's winning ticket for outwitting death.

~

Happy talk keep talking happy talk, Poppa tunes if I look gloomy or just regular. Poppa is the sole survivor of seven children and two parents. Poppa tells me how much I look like his sisters Ruchele and Goldele; not so much like Hafche or Nahche. Poppa sings, *Memories—all alone in the moonlight—*

~

Poppa says to me, *You should become a judge like Deborah in the Bible.* Sometimes Poppa takes me to dance a waltz in the bright sun-yellow kitchen.

Stone for a Pillow

> *God gives Jacob a stone for a pillow. Jacob, alone at night with only a stone for a pillow. On the pillow, then, a vision. Angels ascending and descending a ladder to and from the heavens. —Anonymous Midrash on Genesis 28:11*

Dear God of Abandoned Hope,

I entreat you, may I feel each stone
You place under my head as a bolster
of bright brocade. May my castle
of straw be comely to me.

May You set my bed on the ground
of embodied knowledge. My sometimes-stone
heart, may it soften, forgive my judging mind.
May I be enamored of missteps, mistakes,

lessons hewn from stoneheartedness,
though I know so little how to study,
be curious, remain steadfast, when a heart
closes to me.

And when You, Dear God, extinguish
the sun, drop it below the fiery horizon,
may I see it as night, not as destruction.
May I connect to every closed heart

from a place of belonging. May I know
I am a beam of Your precious light.
I am ladder and rung, cloud and rock
at the same time.

Pillowless

My son doesn't call much, doesn't say
much when he does, but sends clips of Rocky
peaks, prickly cacti, crazy-amazing full splits
and yoga inversions he teaches in a rental with floor
to ceiling windows I look through from his point
of view—the world looks friendlier upside-down.
I miss my son—miss the times he missed
me back, the time the first postcard
from camp read. *I am very very very very sad.*
I guess he has always said exactly enough.

At camp the boy on the next cot kept asking,
Can I have your pillar? Maybe it was one of my son's
sads that this boy had no pillow to hold
his head up. The boys' idol at camp, Daryl
Dawkins, dribbled through his own little boy's legs.
Maybe he'll be a star, Dawkins said.
*But I'm just hoping he'll take care of me
when I'm put out to pasture.
Make me tea. Bring me my pillow.*

I learned young to sleep with one a king-
sized pillow pulled over my ears to block
Poppa's night-terror-sounds. Poppa could speak
five languages enough to not get killed in Poland,
Germany, Russia, Israel, America—Poppa never
got to give his sisters *podushkas*, down
dowries in trade for husbands. Treblinka stole
Poppa's trust, but let him keep his trembling
soft hands. As for Momma—pillowless
years on wood planks in Nazi camps,
so the word *camp* came to mean bones
walking.
   ~
For the month my son was at Sixers Camp,
Momma ends up at Abington Hospital.
Oy, this podushka is a shtyne, this pillow

is a stone. A sheine gilachte. A pretty joke.
So I rush home and bring her my own.
I love and hate giving Momma my pillow
she might die on. Momma nestles her nose
into the down, breathes me in, says,
All I need, mein daughter, I have now.

Winter Sun Entering My Son's Room

a museum to his childhood, stuffed
doggie slippers, felt tongues ready to lick,
spotted leopard we called Mr. Fox.

I don't mean to be nostalgic.
Husband long dead. Son long living
away from home yet keeping his room

as it was, myriad photos with his dad in butterfly
gardens of Costa Rica, on breathless rocky peaks,
his dad's arms reaching toward heaven as if

leaving earth already if it were not for his legs
planted like cypress trees. Planted like mountains,
twenty-two photos in all, each a romance. Husband

kissing our son's baby-boy ebullient cheek,
son's squealing delight I get to hear again and again
when I enter, the sunlight halos.

Momma Would Say *Sara* or *Hella*, Then Turn

her head side to side, look up
        into the blue or billowy sky.

Momma would say, *Sara, her bunker*
        was supposed to be safe.

Sara, so beautiful. Her teeth
        not so straight.

Momma would say, *Hella, too many*
        sores to stay

in the life line. Oy, shtel doh hof. Stand up,
        Momma would invoke

the dead. A sudden crowd
        of starlings comes to roost

in the tulip trees. Never such a symphony
        in Momma's *shtetl.*

I myself am someone comfortable
with tones about one decibel

above the quiet of a library.
Could I be gracious enough, then,

to call it grace, the raucous starlings,
come to visit?

Ancestral spirits
making a racket in the tulip trees.

Last Generation of Men

Poppa in his pale blue suit swept
Momma across the dance floor,
just-right-press of palm to her chiffon back,

a waltz, a tango, a cha-cha, Momma
gladly followed Poppa's scent of Old Spice.
Poppa, last generation of men who knew

how to lead, who smoked Marlboros
with no Surgeon General warning
on the pack's vertical ledge.

Last generation of men who played
poker for nickels and dimes, calling *aces,
deuces and queens running wild*

in the basement while Momma played
gin rummy in the kitchen with *the girls,*
last generation of women who cleaned up
without noticing who was winning.

One moment my life is a stone in me, the next, a star

What I am trying to say is jealousy
does not become me. Yet I am
jealous of those who do not feel
lonely when alone. Once that was me.
Now I am jealous of my recently widowed
friend already invited to Shabbas dinner
by a new beau with white, fly-away
longish hair, good smile, beard scruffy the way
she likes it, while here, I must sink
my tongue into the ice cream of my life,
swim my body through blue water and myriad
friends who come to dine on roasted meats
and warm rolls, and so many calls from well-
wishers, and my brother not surgically challenged
today. One moment my life is a child-
flower made of pastel tissue, (mint green,
butter yellow, shell pink, dusk blue)
held together by an emerald-green pipe cleaner,
layers of petals I opened with my fingers,
plush and ancestral, I used to spend hours
unlonely spreading petals into a frightened/
frightening world.

Stone Prophecy Says

Be broken
ground. Be mud. Clay, moldable, be silt, be luminous,
let the only certainty be (love, be truthful),

be questions
with no answers, questions that come in dreams
even if the dream is a grenade

and a boy being pulled belly-down in a cowboy town,
down a dirt road, the only road that leads
to further questions.

He can't seem to let go of the grenade.
You can't save him.
Trouble yourself

not about the boy. Or the sky.
Trouble yourself
about your state

of awakeness. Sit down in your car with the motor
off, windows open. Breathe
in the leaves. Say nothing

of the rootlessness that comes at such times.
No need to explain
yourself to anyone.

The mind is inconvenient.
It says too much and gives
few true words.

Part 2

Joy doesn't exist without the intolerable. —Ross Gay

Enough Lament

Do I admit I don't lament for the world—enough
lament for my beloved who died on a delightful, warm

October day just before Sabbath's auspicious full moon?
Do I tell you that from his slow and quiet death I learned

to love now and now and now? And kindness is always an option.
Do I admit I admire, but fail to engage in the Buddhist practice

of *tonglen,* inhaling the suffering world, exhaling compassion.
Do I tell you I hoard compassion, afraid I will starve

on bad news? Do I tell you enough lament beneath childhood's
roof for Momma's seven sisters, for Warsaw razed to rubble

and ash, for the 6 million that once seemed a big number?
Do I admit I keep tabs on the numbers dead from COVID less

than those from bullets, from knees choke necks, from brokenness?
Do I admit lament for burnt books and prayer shawls, 500,000

genocided gypsies and fears that cause all *usses* and *thems*?
Do I say yesterday my spiritual teacher opened the zoom floor

for meditators to speak our hearts and a *virtual* fight ensued.
One man said, *Acts of rebellion are necessary for change.*

Another, *My daughter lives beside Sam's deli, shattered glass,
looted shelves, and when she called 911 no one answered.*

Do I admit I turned off the sound so I could stay in the silent
company of my fellow meditators who had just minutes ago

finished a forty-five-minute *tonglen* practice
breathing in pain, breathing out compassion?

Poppa

This morning Poppa enters our canary yellow kitchen, stands at mock attention in his Fruit of the Loom ribbed tank shirt, his Blondie and Dagwood boxer shorts, (the comic strip couple chasing each other with hearts and exclamation marks in cloud bubbles over their heads), and salutes. Poppa puffs his lower lip into a silly pout, closes his smoke blue eyes, turn his big, shiny head left, right, left, then like a happy parrot, he sings, *Morning to you, good morning to you, and a happy Howdy Doody.*

Poppa doesn't notice his Fruit of the Loom are inside-out or that his private parts flop out when he sits down. *Avram, fix yourself!* Momma chides. Dutifully, he tucks himself in, rises, and mock-marches to the fridge. *I need something to wettin' my whistle*, he says. The taste of American expressions pleases him perhaps as much as his apricot-prune compote and grapefruit half he dives into with un-serrated teaspoon. Tart juices spirt.

Ach, Abram, eat like a mensch not like a Chmielniker, Momma scolds, all part of Sunday mornings' sweet ritual. At the mention of Chmielnik, Poppa's eyes wander to a dark time in a dark country. Ragged grapefruit sections slide into his mouth without him noticing. Though Momma reprimands him, I somehow understand his Chmielnik ways also comfort her as well. Both Momma and Poppa from Polish *shtetls,* both survivors of starvation years, concentration camp years, living grave years, Holocaust years, so food in our house, its quantities, portions, urgencies, mean so many things.

After the whistle-wetting, Poppa sits at the yellow and white Formica table like a mock-obedient schoolboy and waits for the doting ceremony to begin. He has of course brought to the table the sacred tube of Alberto VO5 and the serious tortoise shell comb. Momma runs the wide teeth across Poppa's fifty extra-long-to-cover-the-bald-spot hairs making perfectly parallel pitch-black rows. If Poppa gets up before she is done, Momma follows him like a fly on a restless sticky bun. Poppa says, maybe Vaseline is better than Alberto. Cheaper. *Grease is grease.* Momma laughs though she knows Poppa isn't joking. It's his Chmielnik speaking. She calls him *my Alberto.*

Poppa's round head looks extra-large this morning. I love watching this service. Such rapt attention to even rows under Momma's hawk eye. And the earnest way Poppa offers the holy comb to Momma, gives her the honor and pleasure of doting, perfecting, loving him in this particular way.

Decades later, when Poppa is seventy, Momma wishes she could give Poppa a giant sea of grapefruit juices to dive into. But instead, Poppa gets *super alimentation* through a J-tube.

Cousin Arthur comes religiously on Sunday mornings for breakfast and a touch of Torah talk or thought after working night shift in a meat freezer. Arthur grew up with Poppa in Chmielnik, remembers the same rabbi, the same pretty or homely girls forbidden by Torah to be gazed upon, the same forbidden soccer game they both played, the same liquidation of 10,000 Jews from their town that took only three days. The two of them, close in conversation or in silence. This was good, because Poppa can no longer speak or eat like a *Chmielniker* let alone like a *mensch*. His illness has taken so much of him. Momma calls the situation, *a true Holocaust*, Poppa, in his wheelchair, knees barely fitting under the dining table, Momma swabbing Poppa's lips with a mint sponge. Momma losing more weight than Poppa, feeling guilty for eating.

This Sunday morning, Arthur is sitting at the table to Poppa's right, I to Poppa's left. Momma serves sliced rye with herring. Rye at Momma's house is either same-day-fresh or thrown out. Herring at Momma's house is a squat jar placed directly on the table, filled with gray fish, heads intact, slumped in a pool of sour cream.

Poppa stares his Shy Drager Syndrome stare, and when our eyes are not on him, inches a shaky-weak hand toward the sacramental herring jar, dives fingers in, grabs a slippery one, draws it to his lips, sucks it into his mouth and swallows it, hook, line and sinker.

Tell-tale sour cream on his once pouty lips. If his illness allowed his mouth muscles to smile, he would be grinning ear to ear. Poppa has not eaten solid food in over a year. Would he choke after all this time under Momma's hawk-eye? The herring successfully swallowed. Poppa, a triumphant Chmielniker, his blue eyes look up toward heaven. I imagine this to be his salute to the God who has kept him alive to this miraculous day.

Memorial Flame

1.

I just called 911, my son says, absent
of alarm.
I'm sitting in the kitchen eating cheese

Danishes with five women
the way Momma did
with her gin rummy friends.

We've left the living room
after blowing out the full moon
ritual candles.

Now a strangely low, even flame
rises from the woven blanket spread
for the ceremony.

Toppled candle left lit.
Firemen circle the block, miss the house
three times, street numbers

none-sequential.
Firemen cut away
the quenched square of wall-to-wall

fire-resistant blush beneath blanket,
feel the wood floor under both,
Smoldering

fires can hide,
start later
if left unchecked.

2.

Still, street numbers remain
random, dangerously

out of order

until police point firearms
at my front door
thinking my street number

is 1440 until I point
four houses down, too late
to stop

the father from killing
himself after killing
his own son.

The father had called
911 earlier to say,
come. Come now.

3.

Nothing in my life seems to hold
a candle to what Momma told
or hid smoldering.

4.

The hairs in my nostrils,
the tongue in my mouth
remember. It was 1943,

keynote at the Holocaust Memorial says.
Not possible to see the sun
through the smoke

and flames. The smell
of my city burning, I must tell you,
comes back in dreams.

Our children are

our memorial candles,
she says in conclusion.

*Momma, do you remember the smell
of Warsaw burning?* I ask.
Of course, she says, *how could I forget?*

Why have you never mentioned it?
She answers, *What is there left
to say?*

I look at Momma's blue
Auschwitz number tattooed
on her forearm,

number I have failed
to memorize
all these years.

5.

Disembodied arms jut out,
reach up on the rising
memorial, horrified moon

faces of children, also,
braided flames widen and twist
at the top of chaos.

Mind aflame, Rappaport
sketched in thick charcoal,
at our house on Dorcas Street,

first drafts for the sculpture.
Momma and Rappaport, childhood friends
from *Hashomer Hatzair,* Zionist Youth Group

where Momma got called
a coquette for plucking her eyebrows that ran

across her forehead

with no space between, (the way mine do),
where Jewish boys and girls, forbidden to sit
in the same room without a curtain between,

sat side by side scheming
escape Poland to Palestine
or ways to smuggle grenades, meat.

Poppa had more night terrors in Polish
mixed with Yiddish in those months
of charcoal sketches splayed

on our dining table.
In first sketches the braided flames
at the top looked like branches

of the *tree of life*—escaping.

Why I Hate the Word "Horrible" When Used for Less Than

Excerpts from Interview of our mother, Miriam Ferleger, by my brother, David Ferleger, 1998

In 1939 there was the bombing for 3 weeks.
This was the most horrible time.
Every day was a year.
Our cousins, Arthur, Sam, Joseph came to be with us.
We didn't have water in the house.
We had to go to a big lake to get water.
I don't know how we survived.

Never Alone

> *Every little girl needed a doll through which to project herself into her dream of her future* —Ruth Handler, inventor of Barbie Doll

Miss Sievers stands very straight at the classroom door. Of course she's not smiling. The year before, a boy pushed his chair out just to trip her. I know because she was my brother's Kindergarten teacher and my cousin Lilly's too. They were in the same class. Lucky for both of them to have each other. My other cousins are different ages from me, so I am not as lucky.

You know Kindergarten is not compulsory, Miss Sievers explains to Momma. It's my first day back after being sick for a week. *I mean your daughter does not have to be here at all.* Maybe she says this because I sit all by myself at milk and cookies time. Or maybe because we are called the *refs*, which my brother says is short for *refugees*. I only know I love Miss Sievers just for this minute because I'll never see her again. I turn and run really fast out of class, away from Momma and Miss Sievers, into the schoolyard, toward the high fence before Momma catches up. Momma doesn't punish me or make me go back. Momma loves me but speaks not so much English and looks scared. She tells me she ran home once too. From the *umschlag*. Momma says that's where Jews waited for trains to a *work camp*. Momma says it was really *Treblinka*. Which I think means *very terrible*. Momma says she ran home so at least she would not die alone, but with family.

Back home, Momma and I sit on the not-pretty-green porch bench. Her eyes look very big. But she isn't making a sad face. I am making a glad face because we don't have to be *separated* yet. Everything I know about *being separated* is bad. Momma cries when she talks about her sister Hella *getting separated* in the *sick people line in the camps.* Then she *disappeared*. Momma says dead people are safe and they don't ever disappear if you remember them. I picture my disappeared aunts setting the Sabbath table with white dishes, lighting Sabbath candles, or crying in trains like Momma did, or hiding in dark holes like Poppa did.

It's been a whole week since I left Miss Sievers. Momma says the *cockroaches are making a party in the shower-drain* so I can get washed in the sink. Then she says she's going to take umbrellas to my brother and cousin and it's raining too hard for me to walk with her.

After Momma leaves, I count to one-hundred four times, put on my goulashes and my shiny red raincoat, and walk down Wyoming Avenue to Clara Barton Elementary. My brother told me Clara Barton was a nurse with a Red Cross and helped refugees. I know I am going the right way because I pass Bogoslavski's bakery where Momma buys us salt sticks.

The day after I cross the street by myself Momma buys me a Barbie, so I'll never be alone. I dress her in a pink tissue, two tiny holes for her skinny arms to fit through. She sleeps in my pink tissue box with white flowers on it. I wake her and sit her up so she can listen to my first poem, called "My First Friend." She looks happy to hear. My Barbie doesn't have any stories to tell.

First Taste of Salt

My brother was my first crush.
Mornings, I'd watch him pour a pyramid
of salt into his palm, pop it into his mouth,
take a giant bite of buttered-thick seeded-rye

Momma bought at Bogoslafskis one block down,
take a fat swig of OJ fresh-squeezed by Momma
who pressed hard on the silver lever
that made the silver dome bow-down.

As for me, I'd lick the coarse salt grains off a salt stick,
imagine it a salt lick, and I, a chestnut mare
who could whinny and neigh, say exactly
what I wanted just by a toss of my head,

swish of my shiny dark mane. Salt to nourish
my nerve cells, give me courage to trust.
A horse is trustworthy only after you've earned
her trust. Holocaust kids can't trust

who will stay—alive. My brother never entered
my room (though there was an adjoining door),
except once when Momma asked him to teach me
how to tie my shoes.

We sat on the pink linoleum floor decked
with blue diamond shapes I counted each night
instead of sheep. We sat beside my rocking horse.
My horse had a pink saddle, a happy yellow mane.

Somersault Solo in the Senior Expressive Arts Center

I am told to take up
        more space
                on the dance floor. I do

a solo of somersaults leaps slides dizzy free
        from my struggle
                with how much air

to take up with my *my,* my *me,*
        my inbreath, my needs, my
                wants I have always wanted

to cover a whole sheet
        of paper with thick paint
dense brush, big motion

of Van Gogh. No more space for even one
        more stroke of wheat.
                I once touched

his impasto fields though only with one
        finger behind my back
                eyes glued to the guard

who kept scanning the room
        for touchers, vandals, thieves.
                Today is the first day

since the 8th grade I've painted
        anything at all. Back then, red
                carnations filled a cart. Not roses.

I painted as if I knew the cobblestone
        streets of gay Paree
                in another century, mustachioed

vendor under June sun. I longed for my art
        to breathe beside Van Gogh's.
                Mr. Katz hung the contest rules

on the wall. A classmate cracked a mean joke
        on the far side of the room. Mr. Katz,
                face contorted, threw

his hands under the curved faucet
        of the art-sink and splashed us closest
                till one of us wept.

This was not the only reason
        I made myself
                small.

Nothing Is Everything

My brother and I—heirs
to whole cities
razed
to rubble
both of us
heirs to the one
shirt—one
pair of pants
Poppa wore inside
his living
grave—two
or two and a half
years—hard
to know how
long—heir to numb-
nothing
left except
infinite threads
to the fire-
orange-sky
and the
necessity
of light.

Leepah

My Grandfather, Leepah, maternal, stood long-listening
for God—*davened* three times a day in the tiny *shul*, scrubbed,
at 5 am, the family wash against a washboard when no one

watched—a *shtetl* husband not meant to do a *shtetl* wife's work.
My grandfather Leepah, maternal, worried who would marry
his daughters with such scant dowries behind the walls

of the Warsaw Ghetto, Leepah, who never saw a photo
of America, never knew a Black man, never knew of the Black
Ghetto, never dreamed of living anywhere but someplace

safe, or perhaps never dreamed because dreaming for any man
in any ghetto can be too dangerous. I am told when I'm fifty,
my grandfather Leepah stayed behind, body no longer able,

his daughters and wife, tearful or numb, on the run
to the next bunker. Hinde Leah, his wife, mum after that.
How many gasses, guns does it take to kill the same man?

How many witnesses does it take to make genocide true?
How many of our family names has my brother found
on the roll calls of Auschwitz, Majdanek, Bergen Belsen?

How many women armed with garlands have no graves
to put them on? How many headstones stolen
from Jewish graveyards are still steppingstones,

in Prague, in Poland? How many times Poppa stood
in *shul* next to Momma for every Mourner's Kaddish
since neither knew the dates their sisters and parents

were murdered, so any day might be a *Yahrzeit* Day.

Shoppers Guide for the Vilnius Flea Market

> More than 95% of Lithuania's Jewish population was massacred over the 3 year German occupation. —Wikipedia

don't haggle—
they'll think you're alive
jew—don't be
alive or they'll tax you to walk
the dead
jew in your arms
over the bridge you'll go
with the body
you once
licked salty skin
that needs you still
to cover
the dead jew
there are never too many
the guide said
as the dead cannot return
the favor you must
carry on and on
the guide carries on
about the locks
padlocked to the bridge
for good luck
to Polish newlyweds
already lucky they are
not jews whose locks
whose side-locks loved
a bargain for more
breath, my sister can't stop
buying scuffed boots
how she will fit
piles of shoes
into her suitcase
she swears she doesn't ever
think about how she is

a jew she can't stop
haggling three
for the price of one
two jews alive
at the Vilnius flea market
I stand, sentry while my sister squats,
pisses behind a living tree.

The Brain and All Its Parts

Poppa used to delight in grossing me out
by ordering sweetbreads, really the unsweet pancreas

of a cow, or caramelized calf-brains with capers,
delicacies I couldn't believe could be kosher, foods

Poppa, in his dirt road *shtetl life*, surely didn't dine on.
Yet here in this land of free and refugee, Poppa splurged

to heal his war years of raw potatoes and piss.
Imago therapy claims to heal young wounds.

This week, in Imago class we pore over power-points:
amygdala, gyrus cingulate, hippocampus,

but each time I take a quiz, I get new things wrong,
feel anxious, unworthy for not remembering

what part of my brain tastes the hard pulp
of raw potatoes Poppa ate in his hiding place

underground, or meager meat sneaked to Momma,
by her father under the table in the Warsaw Ghetto,

as if my parents' mouths were mine.
What part of my brain still sings, sixty years later,

Momma's *iy loo-loo-loo baby* song to the dog
to calm him while I comb out his knots.

What part feels Momma's fingers as if
she still spreads my waist-long hair into a fan

above my head on her bed, brushes out my *plontofs*
with one hand, the other pressed at the roots

so it doesn't hurt so much. What part forgets touch
from Momma that felt relaxed, easy—I forgive her.

It was Momma who taught me forgiveness.
Never go to bed angry because you never know

who will be left alive in the morning. Her whole brain touched,
(Poppa's too,) by genocide's lack of tenderness.

The Egg Trick

1.
1945, Poppa bartered Black Market cigarettes for Black Market eggs,
gave six to Momma who gave two to each surviving sister, one who
cooked hers, the other who broke her eggs onto cement, *better to starve,*
said her fear of Poles still ready to kill a Jew, especially one with golden eggs.

1953, Poppa loved Sundays to cook up twelve eggs for us six cousins.
Some batches with butter, some without, catering to the wishes of each,
scrapies for some, mushy for others. I didn't yet understand it was Poppa's
triumphant way to strip the cold wings from the Angel of Death.

2.
1983, on the TV screen, Momma and I watch a craggy, *babushked*
peasant woman point her sad arthritic crooked finger at a field
behind her house in Bransk, saying, *Neighbors sold news of Jews'
hiding places to Nazis in exchange for a little salt, a stick of butter.*

Momma says to me, *Why are you crying? Yes of course,* Momma says,
*Polish people did those things. Good things and bad things, they did.
Of course the Babcha is afraid to say which neighbors.
Of course. Everyone is still afraid.*

I don't ask Momma why she thinks the Polish farmer didn't sell
Poppa out. Why the farmer kept Poppa hidden in a hole over two years,
never told his boys, (too dangerous), why each night told them he was going
to the barn to feed the pigs. Why he dropped precious potatoes down to Poppa.

3.
Momma would have been too grief stricken to understand
she had raised a daughter with war's nervous system wired
throughout her body. It was no one's fault, my long-ago
too much food, my long-ago resistance movement

around food, especially the un-eating of it. To survive
on so little, prove I could be like Poppa and Momma, last,
endure. Perhaps it felt triumphant, safe, as if I was breaking
on cement all the golden eggs given to me.

4.
I grew up with two extra mothers, my dear aunts,
the one who broke her two eggs, the one who cooked hers.
I grew up believing I was keeping the grown-ups
on edge, always on edge. Edges everywhere.

Momma Speaks of Her Father, Leepah

Excerpts from Interview of our mother, Miriam Ferleger, by my brother, David Ferleger, 1998

Daddy, my father, was always in the kitchen. When we had the…how do you call it? When you washed clothes, you know, you'd boil the clothes. It was a whole production. It was from wood, a big thing to wash clothes. It wasn't a wringer, but with the hands. So daddy was ashamed to go in, to do this. After all, you know, for him to be dealing with clothes wasn't so nice, so he got up at 5:00 in the morning so mother shouldn't see him doing this.

~

I was so proud to walk with him in the street. I was holding his hand, you know. One time we had an argument. I wanted ice cream in the middle of the night. I decided I wanted ice cream, and he said no, and I thought this was terrible, because he was never angry.

~

My mother always used to say that he was so lucky that, without words she knows he was like the king for us. He did things for you, but he never gave you real lectures. He was very quiet. And he was gorgeous. I remember I had one girlfriend. She used to say, "I'm coming over to look at your father." I swear to God. I'll never forget this. When he walked into a room, you really had to turn around to look at him, because he was tall, with a long beard and beautiful eyes and very gorgeous hands. I don't know. I always kissed them. I know that.

Summer Says

Pay attention to
your heat, your survival—

the tree is a sequined
vernacular, a cashmere sweater

because nothing matters in the end
but tenderness

and the bending light.

Summer says, I will be the room you die in.
You will dream,

neither of regret, nor in the language
you were born into.

You will stop accusing
those you love

of lack.
You ask, what is the past?

What is it all for? Summer says,
the wound of being untaught.

Summer says the cypress is a hospice.
Summer says, falter, falter, falter,

bloom, bloom, bloom—

There Is the Smell

of Japanese beetles burning under my brother's magnifying glass,
under August sun. Gemstone blue-green wings that crunched.

There is the smell of Momma's beehive hairspray and Estee
Lauder. The smell of my best friend Norit's blue pills and black

coffee mouth and her momma's flat expression as she draped
Norit's arm around my neck, directed me in her broken

English, to walk Norit in circles to keep her from dying
from something called *an overdose*.

There is the smell of fourteen and best friends before I knew
what it meant to love. There is the smell of bodies

being dragged across the black & white TV screen
in Norit's drab paneled basement. The smell of her father's

Eau Pour L'Homme and his boyish laugh. Smell of *coorva*,
Hebrew for *whore* he called Norit for kissing

an eager boy in the basement. Smell of the basement
where we played *Life*, the board game. Smell of sheets

of rain meeting the green grasses. Smell of mint
in the garden—breaking open a leaf.

At Ghost Ranch

1.

Every strand of hair sings
of sage even as you fly back east,
and the star-saturated sky erases any sense
of self-importance, and the Milky Way
makes you bow down no matter how
many of your tribe have vanished.

2.

If you drive south toward Tularosa
you see bald mesas ringed with sky-
blue, pink and teal pastels that play
on the stereo of sunlight. And deep purses
of land called *bolsons* fill with ephemeral bodies
of water in deluge season, and when the rain
is spent, and the sun swallows up the lakes,

what's left are acres of salt and milk-
white and bone-white and talc-white
lizards and snakes and geckos
that run up and down tree trunks
and rest on white stucco walls.
Invisibly, they survive, sun themselves.

3.

But if you stay at Ghost Ranch
you may hear the tick-tick-ticking
in my chest. Never mind. You have your own
crow sounds, caws in the sunlight follow you.
I do not have anything to teach you.
I have only this cracked blue mirror.

What is it that shakes your cells?
Is it the Pueblo ghosts leaving and entering

Box Canyon at will? Or fear of seeing
a black cow flying over it?
Legend says no one can see her
without dying on the spot.

4.

In these ghost lands
I miss those I love
back home. When I leave,
I will miss red crumbling shale,
carved bird heads, beaks swelling
against canyon walls.

5.

I will miss the Pueblo woman
with coal eyes, who says she could
live on unfiltered river water and the juice
of cactus.

I used to try to live on meager meat
to prove myself a survivor.
Like Momma.

Momma who lived years on
a bowl of weak broth, slice of bread,
sliver of hope.

Notes:

Daven: In Judaism reciting the required liturgical prayers in Hebrew. (https://languages.oup.com/google-dictionary-en/OxfordLanguages Dictionary)

Majdanek: First concentration camp/extermination camp my mother was sent to with her two surviving sisters. Majdanek was a Nazi concentration and extermination camp located outside Lublin, Poland during World War II where Jews were murdered on an industrial scale as part of Operation Reinhard, the Nazi *plan to murder all Polish Jews in German-occupied Poland*. (https://en.wikipedia.org/wiki/The_Holocaust_in_Poland)

Mein: Transliteration for the Yiddish word for *my*.

Peyos: Hebrew word that refers to sidelocks or unshorn sideburns Orthodox Jewish men and boys wear for religious reasons based on an interpretation of the Hebrew Bible's rule against shaving the sides of one's head. Hebrew word literally means *sides*. (https://en.wikipedia.org/wiki/The_Holocaust_in_Poland)

Plontofs: Polish word for *knots*.

Shoah: Hebrew word for *catastrophe*. Shoah specifically refers to the planned and executed mass killing of nearly six million Jews in Europe by Nazi Germany and its collaborators during WW II, 1941–1945. (https://en.wikipedia.org/wiki/The_Holocaust_in_Poland)

Shtetl: Yiddish word for any pre-war Jewish village or small town in Eastern Europe.

Tonglen: Tibetan Buddhist practice of sending and receiving using the breath, sending out compassion with the exhale.

Treblinka: Nazi concentration and extermination camp near Warsaw, Poland. Between 1942-1945 an estimated 700,000-900,000 Jews were murdered in its gas chambers. (https://en.wikipedia.org/wiki/The_Holocaust_in_Poland) My father's family were transported to this camp and did not survive.

Umschlag: German word means *cargo-handling* or ironically, *sudden change.* (https://en.wikipedia.org/wiki/The_Holocaust_in_Poland)

Umschlagplatz: German word meaning *re-loading place.* During the Holocaust the word referred to a place near a railway station where ghetto Jews were assembled for deportation to death camps. My mother referred to this place as just the *Umschlag.* (https://en.wikipedia.org/wiki/The_Holocaust_in_Poland)

Acknowledgements

Grateful acknowledgements to the following literary journals where some of the poems in this book have been published or will soon appear.

Euphony
    "Shoppers Guide for the Vilnius Flea Market"

Inflectionist Review
    "Love Letter from Time"

L.A. Review
    "When the Night Is Near as a Bird"

Meadow
    "Pandemic Conversations with My Grown Son 1742 Miles Away"

Mizmor
    "*Tashlich*" published under the poem title "Crusts of Our Afflictions"

Offerings: Tiferet Spiritual Poetry Anthology
    "One moment my life is a stone in me, the next, a star"

Sanskrit Literary Arts Journal
    "Be Happy and Never Forget"

Doris Ferleger, Ph.D., a former poet Laureate of Montgomery County PA, is the author of four full length volumes entitled: *Big Silences in a Year of Rain, As the Moon Has Breath, Leavened*, and *As for the Kiss,* and a chapbook entitled *When You Become Snow*. Her work has won numerous awards including New Letters Poetry Prize, Robert Fraser Poetry Prize, Songs of Eretz Poetry Prize, and *AROHO* Creative Non-Fiction Prize, among others. Her most recent book, entitled *As for the Kiss,* published by *Main Street Rag*, was a finalist for Marsh Hawk Poetry Prize and Cod Hill Poetry Prize. Ferleger's work has been published in numerous journals including *Cimarron Review, L.A. Review, South Carolina Review* and *Poet Lore*. She holds an MFA in Poetry and a Ph.D. in psychology. She has studied poetry at Bread Loaf, Colrain, and at Literary Seminars, in Sicily, Lithuania and Poland. and in writers residencies under the tutelage of Terrance Hayes and Natalie Goldberg, among others. Ferleger maintains a psychotherapy practice informed by her trainings in *Imago* and *Real Dialogue Therapy* as well as *Non-Dual Healing.* Among many accolades about her poetry, Aliki Barnestone writes: *These memorable poems keep singing with their insistent beauty.*

www.ingramcontent.com/pod-product-compliance
Lightning Source LLC
Chambersburg PA
CBHW020933180426
43192CB00036B/1139